Things to MAKE and doodle

First published in Great Britain by Buster Books,
an imprint of Michael O'Mara Books Limited, 2011

First published in the United States by Running Press Book Publishers, 2012

Printed in China

Books published by Running Press are available at special discounts for bulk purchases in the United States by corporations, institutions, and other organizations. For more information, please contact the Special Markets Department at the Perseus Books Group, 2300 Chestnut Street, Suite 200, Philadelphia, PA 19103, or call (800) 810-4145, ext. 5000, or e-mail special.markets@perseusbooks.com.

ISBN 978-0-7624-4289-8

9   8   7   6   5   4   3
Digit on the right indicates the number of this printing

Interior design by Barbara Ward
Edited by Hannah Cohen

This edition published by Running Press Kids,
An Imprint of Running Press Book Publishers
A Member of the Perseus Books Group
2300 Chestnut Street
Philadelphia, PA 19103–4371

Visit us on the web!
www.runningpress.com

Things to MAKE and doodle

Exciting Projects to Color, Cut, and Create

by Tony Payne

RP|KIDS
PHILADELPHIA · LONDON

Contents

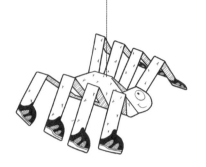

All About This Book

In this book there are lots of cool, crafty creations to cut out and complete. Read on to discover how to complete the doodles and finish the paper projects.

HOW TO BEGIN

1. On each right-hand page you will find the outlines of a new paper project for you to create.

First, turn the page and doodle a cool design on each of the shapes. Sometimes there will be doodling to be done on both sides of the page.

You can use colored pencils or felt-tip pens to complete and color your creations.

2. Once you've finished doodling, turn the page back again.

3. Now cut out each paper shape roughly, being careful to keep well away from the solid outside edges—this will make it easier to cut the pieces out neatly later on.

Make sure you keep all the instructions safe after you have finished cutting out. You will need these to help you make your paper project.

4. Finally, follow the step-by-step instructions to cut out your crafty creations and bring them to life!

CAREFUL CUTTING

 Always cut out the shapes on the right-hand page—the side of the page on which you see this scissors picture.

This is will ensure your final models don't have black lines showing around the edges.

Only cut along the solid lines that look like this: ———————

To cut out a shape, you will need to master how to hold scissors correctly. First, hold the paper you are cutting in one hand and the scissors in the other.

Then push your thumb through the smaller hole in the handle of the scissors and your middle finger through the larger hole.

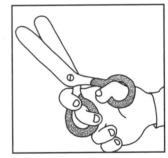

Finally, wrap your index finger around the front of the larger handle, as shown above.

Hold the scissors straight in this position as you cut along a line.

ASK AN ADULT
Cutting out each paper project can be quite tricky, so ask an adult to help if you need to.

SCORING SENSE

"Scoring" along a fold line creates a sharper crease, which helps each paper project to keep its shape or stand up by itself.

To score along a fold line, place a ruler along it and run an old ballpoint pen that has run out of ink along the edge, as shown here.

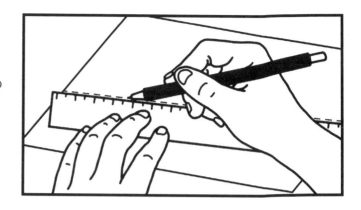

FOLDING RULES

There are two different types of fold lines in this book.

Lines that look like this: ·– – – – – – – – must be folded in a V-shape along the line, so that the fold line is inside the fold.

Lines that look like this: ·– · – · – · – · are reverse fold lines and should be folded in the opposite direction, so that the fold line is on the outside of the fold.

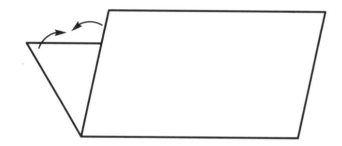

ASK AN ADULT
Folding the paper projects in the right direction can be quite tricky. Ask an adult if you need help.

GLUE AREAS

These dark gray shaded areas show you where to put glue.

Glue area

Always apply a small dab of glue using a glue stick, then press the glued area firmly on to the paper, where marked.

Leave each paper project to dry completely before playing with it.

The light gray shaded areas show you where to stick down the glued area.

Glue positioning area

Big-Cat Straw-Toppers

Turn the page over and doodle your designs, then cut out your toppers below. You will also need two drinking straws.

1. Cut out each topper along the solid outside line, then score along the fold line.

2. Fold each topper in half so that the design is on the inside, then cut out the shaded areas.

Shaded area

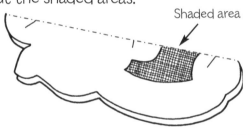

3. While your topper is still folded, make three little cuts, where shown.

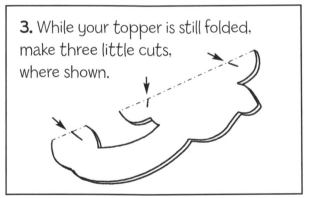

4. Unfold each topper so that the design is on the outside, then thread it on to a straw.

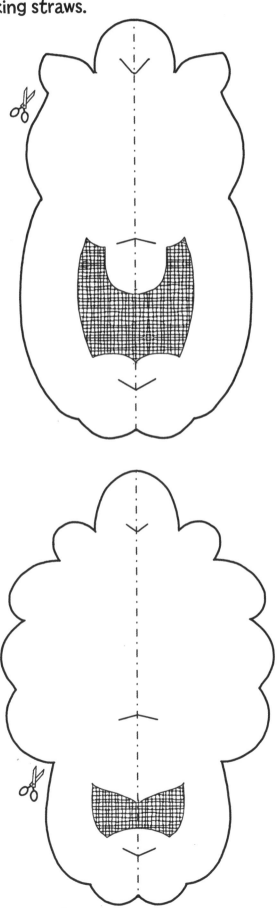

Big-Cat Straw-Toppers

Why not give one big-cat straw-topper to a friend and keep the other for yourself?
Next time you see each other you can slurp in style together!

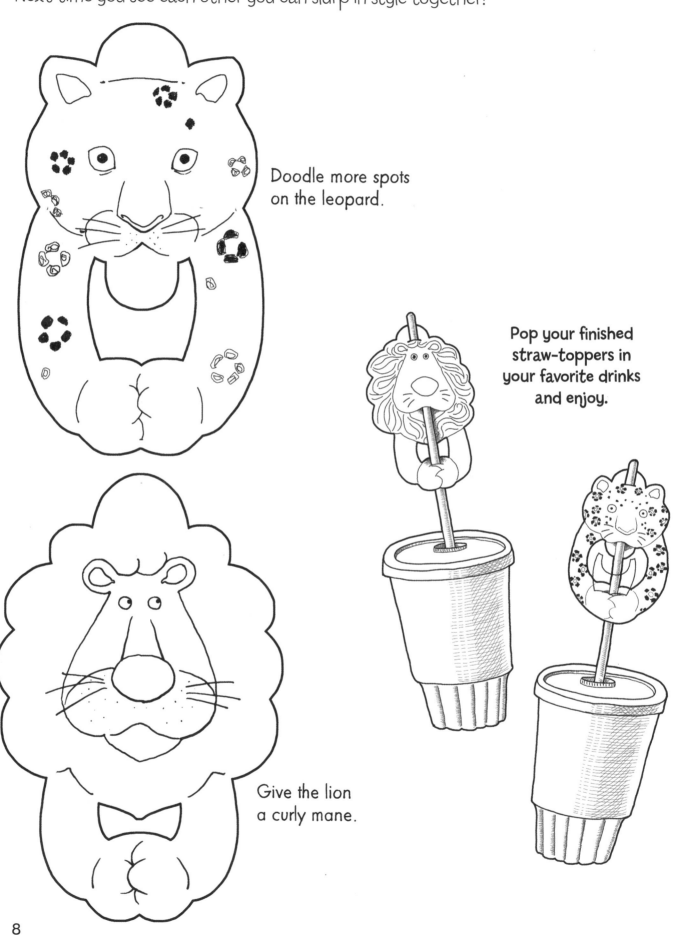

Doodle more spots on the leopard.

Pop your finished straw-toppers in your favorite drinks and enjoy.

Give the lion a curly mane.

Flowerpot Fun

Finish the doodle designs on this page and the next, then cut out the shapes below.

1. Cut out both shapes along the solid outside line, then score along each of the fold lines.

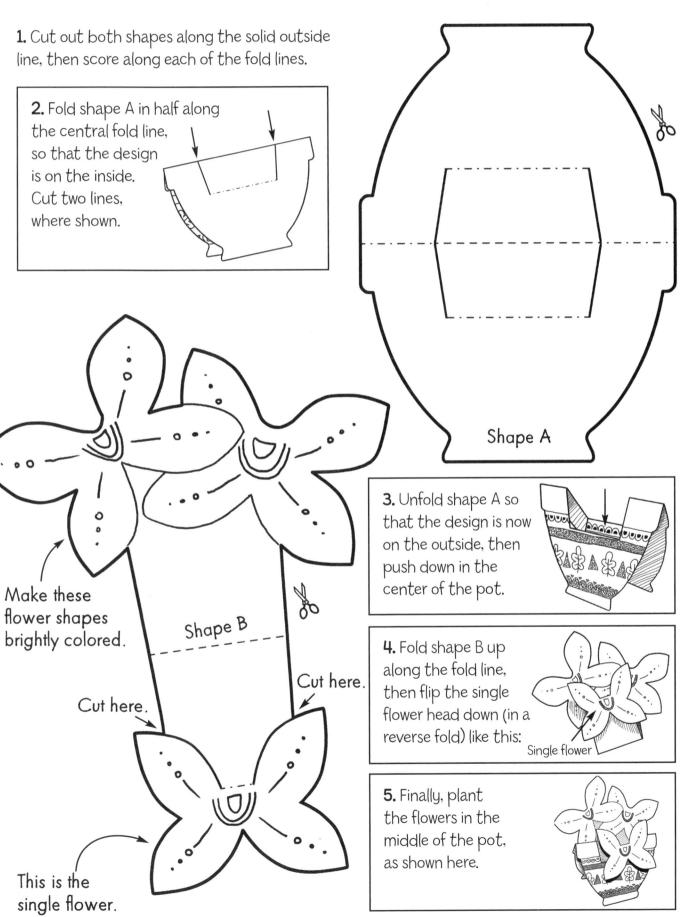

2. Fold shape A in half along the central fold line, so that the design is on the inside. Cut two lines, where shown.

Shape A

Make these flower shapes brightly colored.

Shape B

Cut here.

Cut here.

This is the single flower.

3. Unfold shape A so that the design is now on the outside, then push down in the center of the pot.

4. Fold shape B up along the fold line, then flip the single flower head down (in a reverse fold) like this:

Single flower

5. Finally, plant the flowers in the middle of the pot, as shown here.

Flowerpot Fun

Place your brightly colored pot of flowers on a sunny windowsill—these flowers will stay in bloom forever.

Finished flowerpot

Finish the cool design on this side of the pot and color it in.

Color these flower shapes in bright, beautiful colors.

10

Funny Friend

Turn the page and doodle your design, then cut out your funny friend below.

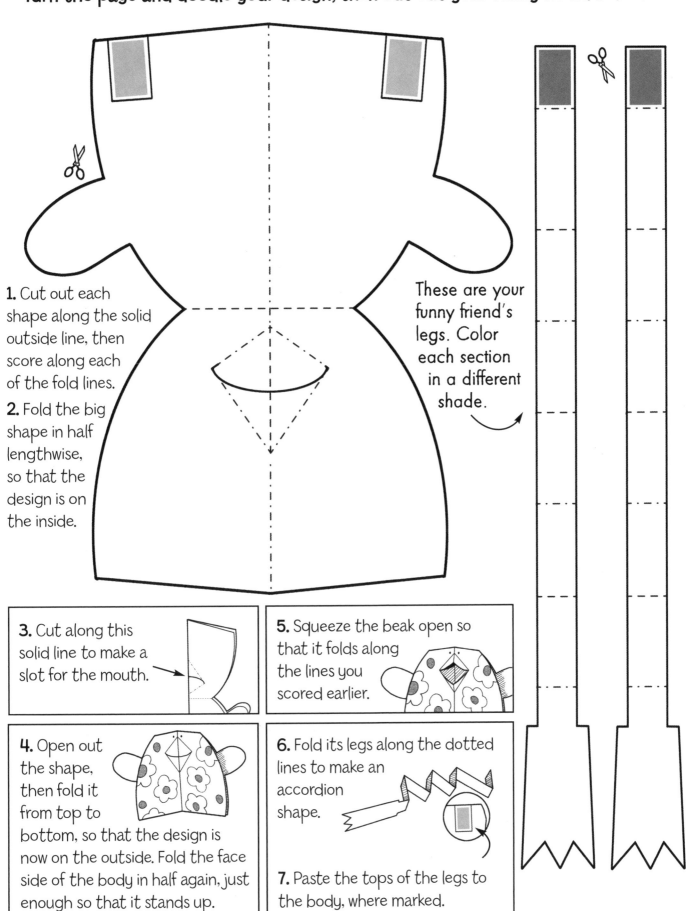

1. Cut out each shape along the solid outside line, then score along each of the fold lines.

2. Fold the big shape in half lengthwise, so that the design is on the inside.

These are your funny friend's legs. Color each section in a different shade.

3. Cut along this solid line to make a slot for the mouth.

4. Open out the shape, then fold it from top to bottom, so that the design is now on the outside. Fold the face side of the body in half again, just enough so that it stands up.

5. Squeeze the beak open so that it folds along the lines you scored earlier.

6. Fold its legs along the dotted lines to make an accordion shape.

7. Paste the tops of the legs to the body, where marked.

Funny Friend

This funny friend sits perfectly on a desk, a shelf, or a bedside table, to keep you company and brighten up your day.

Give it a bright, yellow mouth.

Cover its body in a crazy flower pattern.

Color each panel of its legs in a different color. Give it bright yellow feet, too.

When you turn the page, color in the other side of its legs and feet as well.

Finished funny friend perched on a shelf

Spotty Frog

Finish the doodle design on this page and the next, then cut out your frog below.

1. Cut out the shape along the solid outside line, then score along each of the fold lines.

2. Fold it in half lengthwise, so that the design is on the inside, and cut a slot for its mouth, as marked.

3. Pinch along the diagonal lines around the mouth, then open the shape out. Refold across the middle, so that the design side is on the outside and the frog is facing you. Push its mouth out, so that it looks open.

4. Fold the frog's body inward until it stands up by itself.

5. Fold the arms down over the frog's body, as shown here.

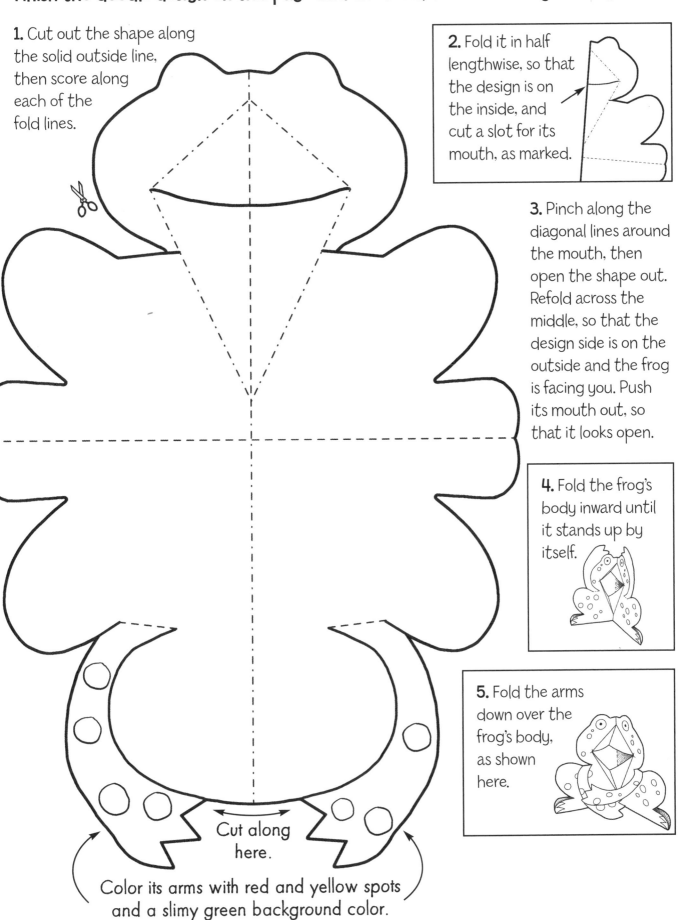

Cut along here.

Color its arms with red and yellow spots and a slimy green background color.

Spotty Frog

Some frogs have brightly colored spots on their skin so that their enemies think that they won't taste nice or might be poisonous.

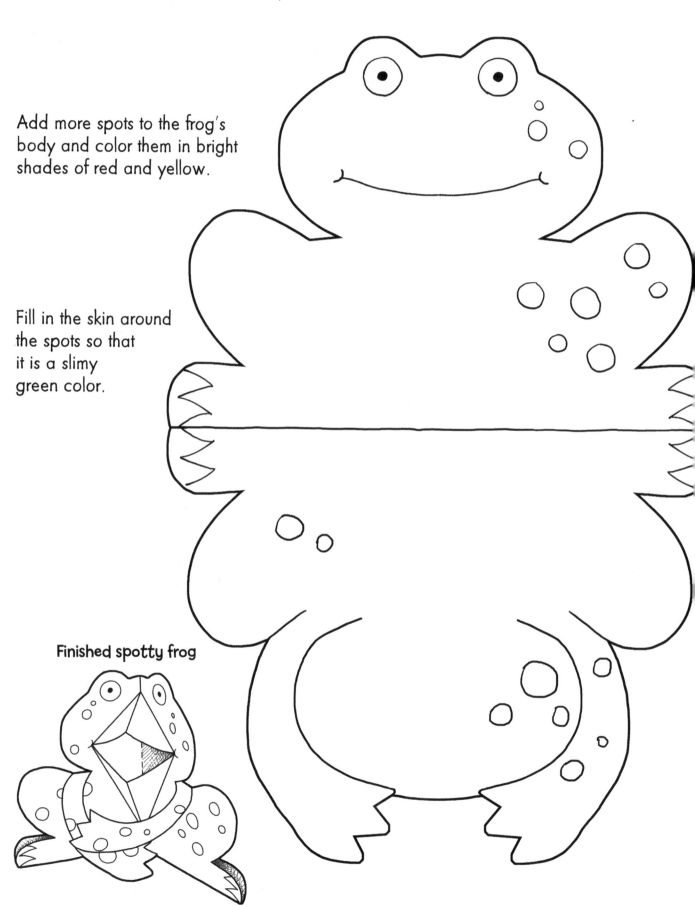

Add more spots to the frog's body and color them in bright shades of red and yellow.

Fill in the skin around the spots so that it is a slimy green color.

Finished spotty frog

Wizard Pen Holder

Turn the page and doodle your design, then cut out your pen holder below.

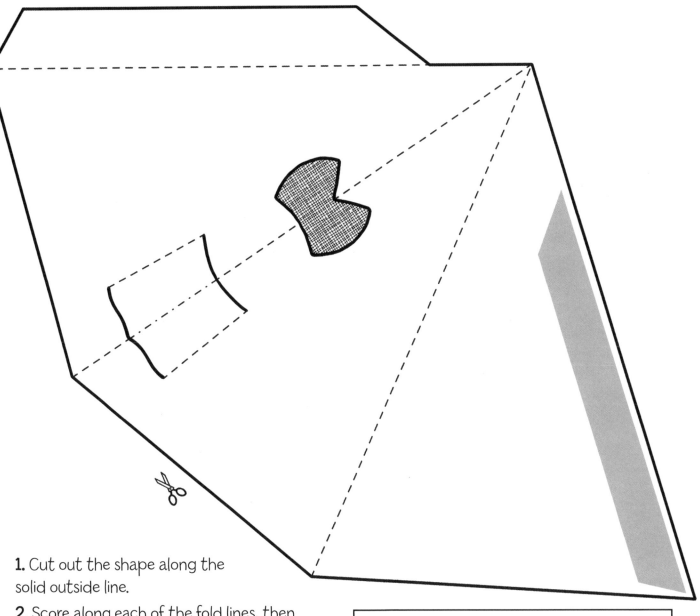

1. Cut out the shape along the solid outside line.

2. Score along each of the fold lines, then fold the shape along the middle fold line, making sure the design is on the inside.

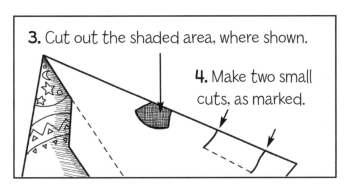

3. Cut out the shaded area, where shown.

4. Make two small cuts, as marked.

5. Open out the shape so that the design is on the outside, then fold it into a pyramid shape.

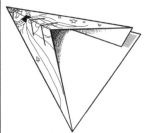

6. Dab some glue on to the tab, where marked, then fix it to the back wall of the pyramid shape.

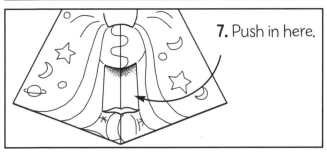

7. Push in here.

Wizard Pen Holder

Keep your wizard pen holder on your desk at home and give him your favorite pen to hold.

Doodle a wizard cape design filled with stars and planets.

Thread a pen through your wizard's hands like this.

Finished wizard pen holder

Terrific Tortoise

Turn the page and doodle your design, then cut out your tortoise below.

1. Cut out the shape along the solid outside line, then score along each of the fold lines.

2. Fold it in half lengthwise along the central fold line, so that the design is on the outside.

3. Fold the back legs so they look like this.

5. Repeat step **4** at the tail end. Then fold up the neck and the tail along the reverse fold lines.

4. Push in the neck along the diagonal fold lines nearest to the center of the shell.

6. Pinch the whole body closed to sharpen up the creases and make it stand properly.

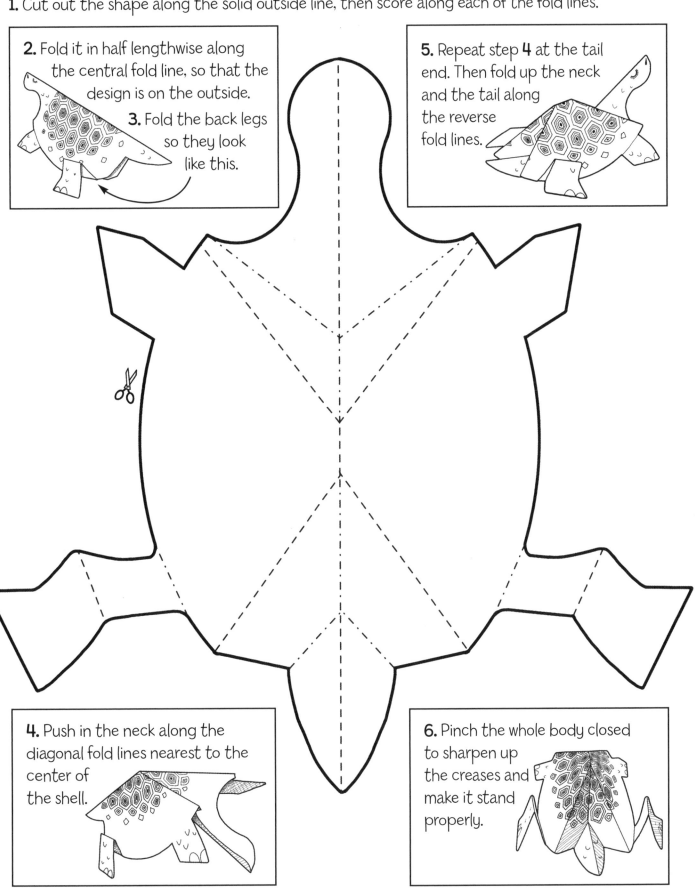

Terrific Tortoise

A tortoise's shell is made of hard, bony plates that protect it from being eaten by hungry predators.

Finished tortoise

Complete this terrific pattern of plates on the rest of the tortoise's shell.

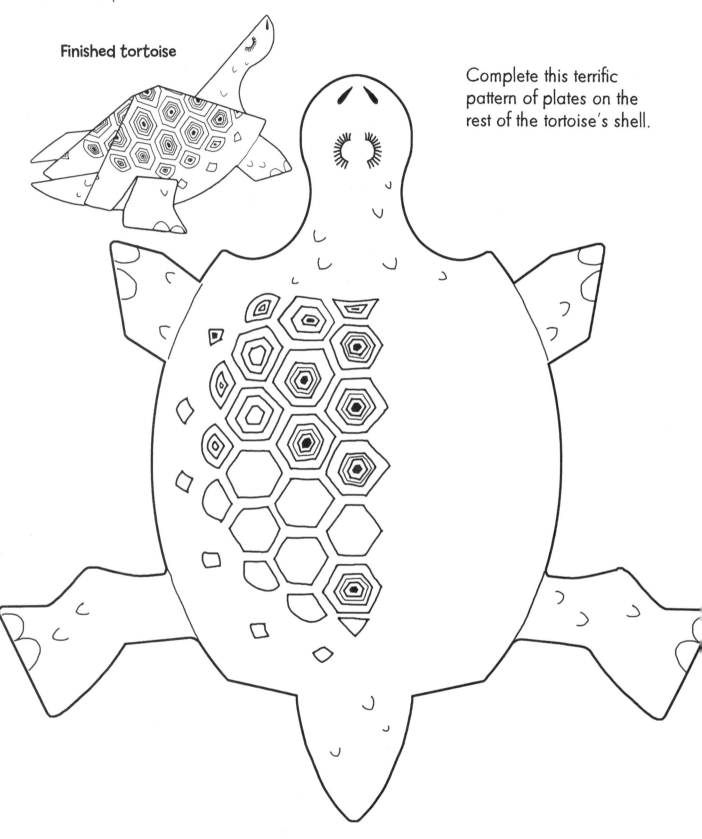

Giant Giraffe

Turn the page and doodle your design, then cut out your giraffe below.

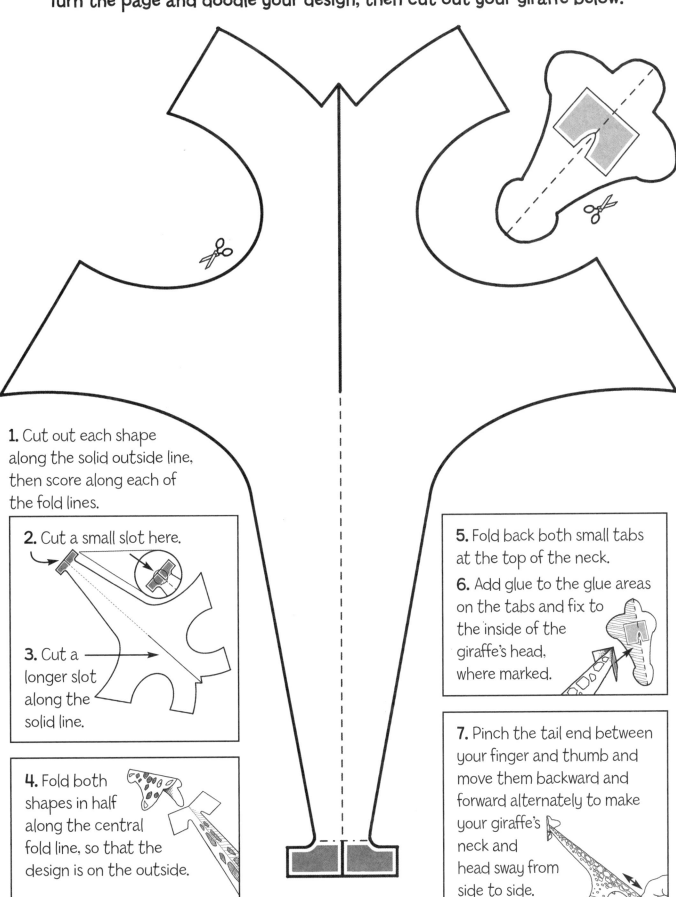

1. Cut out each shape along the solid outside line, then score along each of the fold lines.

2. Cut a small slot here.

3. Cut a longer slot along the solid line.

4. Fold both shapes in half along the central fold line, so that the design is on the outside.

5. Fold back both small tabs at the top of the neck.

6. Add glue to the glue areas on the tabs and fix to the inside of the giraffe's head, where marked.

7. Pinch the tail end between your finger and thumb and move them backward and forward alternately to make your giraffe's neck and head sway from side to side.

Giant Giraffe

Some scientists believe that giraffes have long necks to help them reach for food in tall trees. Others believe that they use their long necks as weapons to fight off rival giraffes.

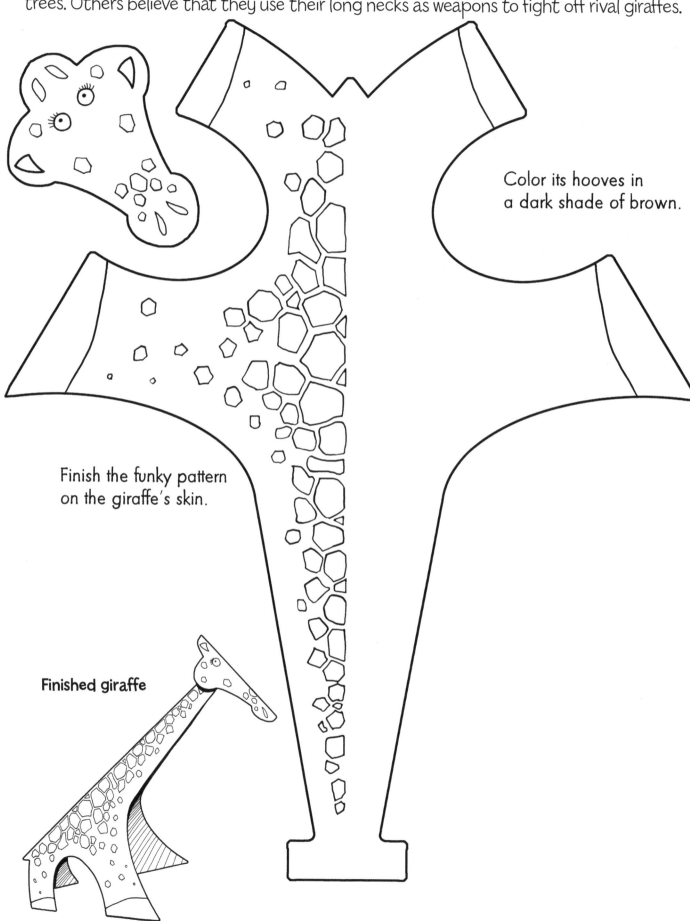

Color its hooves in a dark shade of brown.

Finish the funky pattern on the giraffe's skin.

Finished giraffe

Awesome Owl

Turn the page and doodle your design, then cut out your owl below.

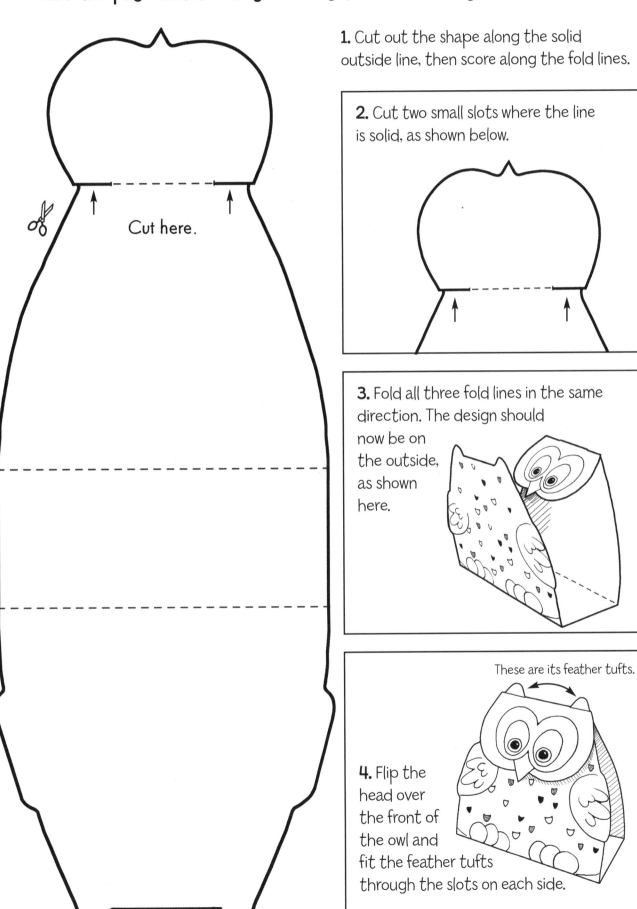

Cut here.

1. Cut out the shape along the solid outside line, then score along the fold lines.

2. Cut two small slots where the line is solid, as shown below.

3. Fold all three fold lines in the same direction. The design should now be on the outside, as shown here.

These are its feather tufts.

4. Flip the head over the front of the owl and fit the feather tufts through the slots on each side.

Awesome Owl

Owls hunt for their prey at night. They have special feathers so that they can fly silently without warning their prey.

Make its big eyes bright yellow.

Finished owl

Add more fluffy feathers and color them in shades of brown and red.

Slithery Snake Mobile

Finish the doodle design on this page and the next, then cut out your snake below. You will also need a length of thread, measuring roughly 12 inches, and some sticky tape.

Color in the zigzag pattern on the snake's body in bright, crazy colors.

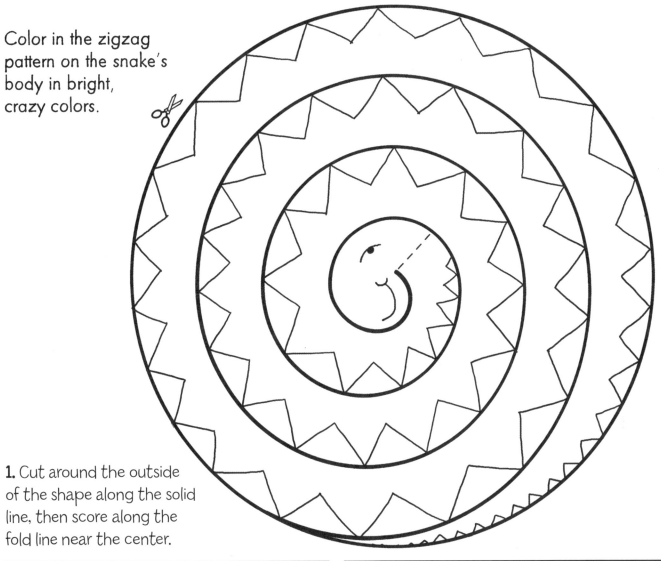

1. Cut around the outside of the shape along the solid line, then score along the fold line near the center.

2. Now cut along the thick, solid spiral line to the center.

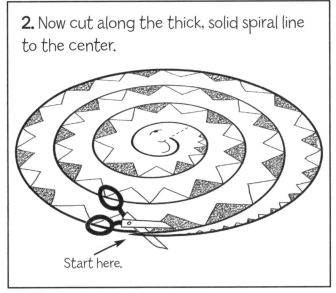

Start here.

3. Bend up the head shape at the fold line and use sticky tape to fix the thread just above the snake's eye.

4. Lift up the thread to uncoil the slithery snake and ask an adult to hang your finished mobile from the ceiling of your bedroom.

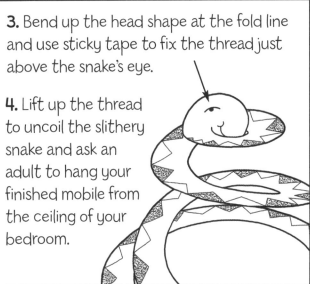

Slithery Snake Mobile

Snake skins are covered with scales, which help them to slither along the ground. As they grow, they shed their outgrown skin to reveal new skin underneath.

Complete the snake with a cool zigzag pattern and color its body in crazy colors.

Finished snakes

Party Place Settings

Finish the doodle designs on this page and the next, then cut out your party place settings below.

1. Cut out each butterfly shape along the solid outside line.

2. Score along each fold line, then fold each shape in half along its fold line, keeping the butterfly's face on the inside.

3. Cut out the shaded areas on each shape, where shown.

4. Open and refold each shape, so that the face is now on the outside.

Complete the dotty designs on these butterflies' wings.

5. Carefully slot each butterfly on to the rim of a glass or cup.

Party Place Settings

Having a party? Write the names of each of your party guests, where marked, on these pretty place settings, then slot each butterfly on to the rim of their cup.

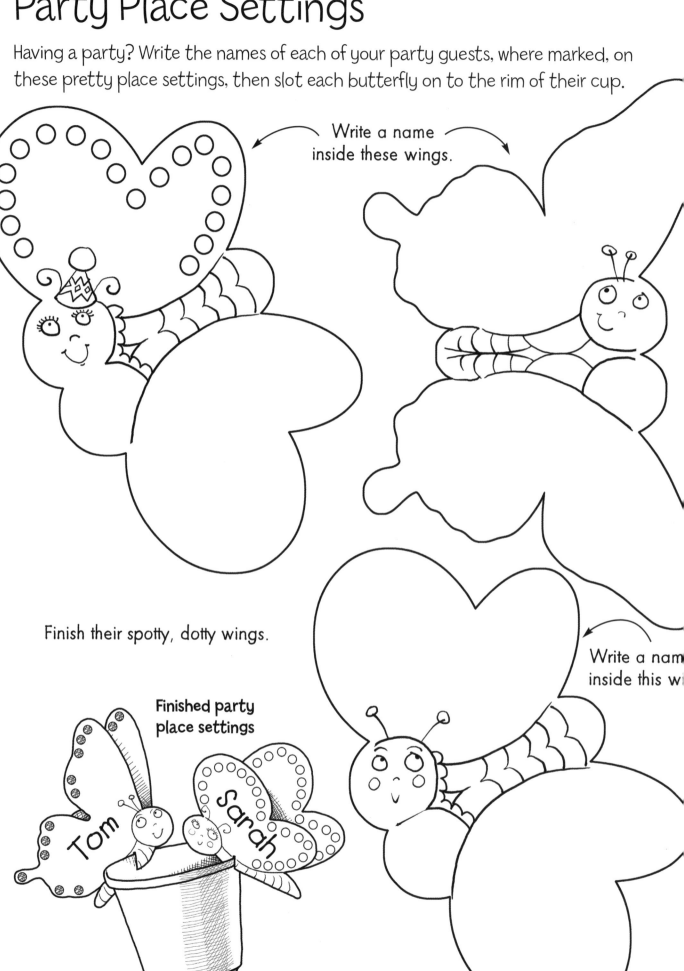

Write a name inside these wings.

Finish their spotty, dotty wings.

Finished party place settings

Tom

Sarah

Write a name inside this wing.

Paper Cracker Snapper

Turn the page and doodle your design, then cut out your snapper below.

1. Cut out these shapes along the solid outside lines.

2. On both shapes, score along each of the fold lines. Next, fold both long edges on each shape inward once to meet at the center.

3. Fold both strips down the middle. The design should now be showing on both sides of both strips.

4. Lay the two folded strips on top of each other and tape the ends together. Separate the two halves like this.

Wind sticky tape around both ends here.

5. Pull the ends sharply apart in the direction of the shorter arrows to make a loud CRACK!

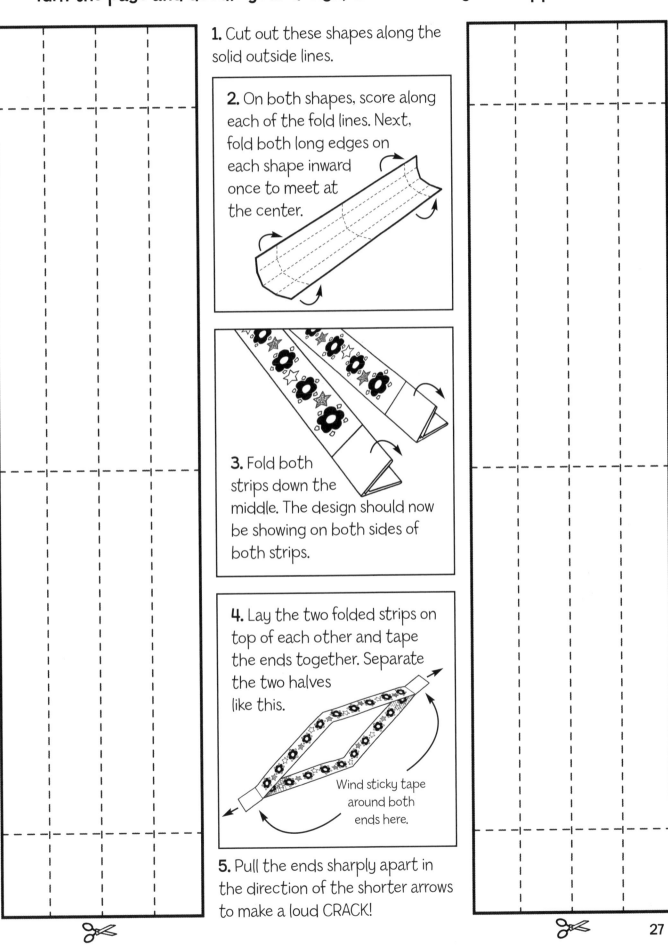

Paper Cracker Snapper

You can practice snapping this paper cracker snapper until you can make a really loud crack.

Fill each strip with a funky flower and star pattern.

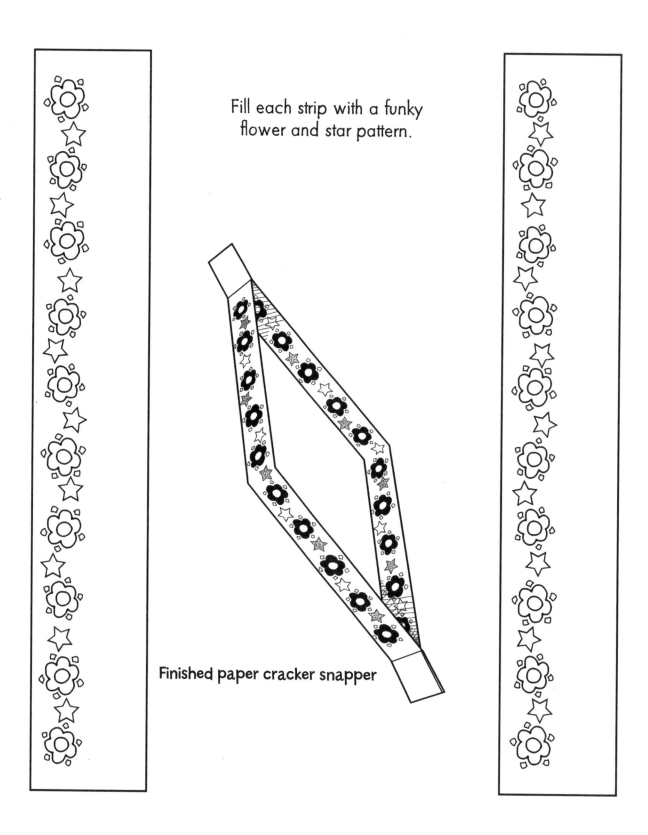

Finished paper cracker snapper

Sparkly Crown

Turn the page and doodle your design, then cut out your crown below.

Shape A

1. Cut out these shapes along the solid outside line, then score along each fold line.

2. Fold shape A lengthwise along the central fold line, with the design on the inside, then cut out the shaded areas.

3. Open and refold shape A so that the design is now on the outside. Dab some glue, where marked, then join the ends together to create a ring.

4. Slot one end of one of the shape B strips between the crown's double layer, then slot the other end into the opposite side.

5. Do the same with the other strip so that it crosses over the first, as shown here.

6. Fold shape C in half along the central fold line, then fold it up and glue the tabs to the very top of the crown.

Shape B

Shape B

Cut along this line, too.

Tab Shape C Tab

Sparkly Crown

When you've finished making this super sparkly crown, why not crown your favorite toy with it?

Cover each of these shapes in sparkling jewels and precious gem shapes.

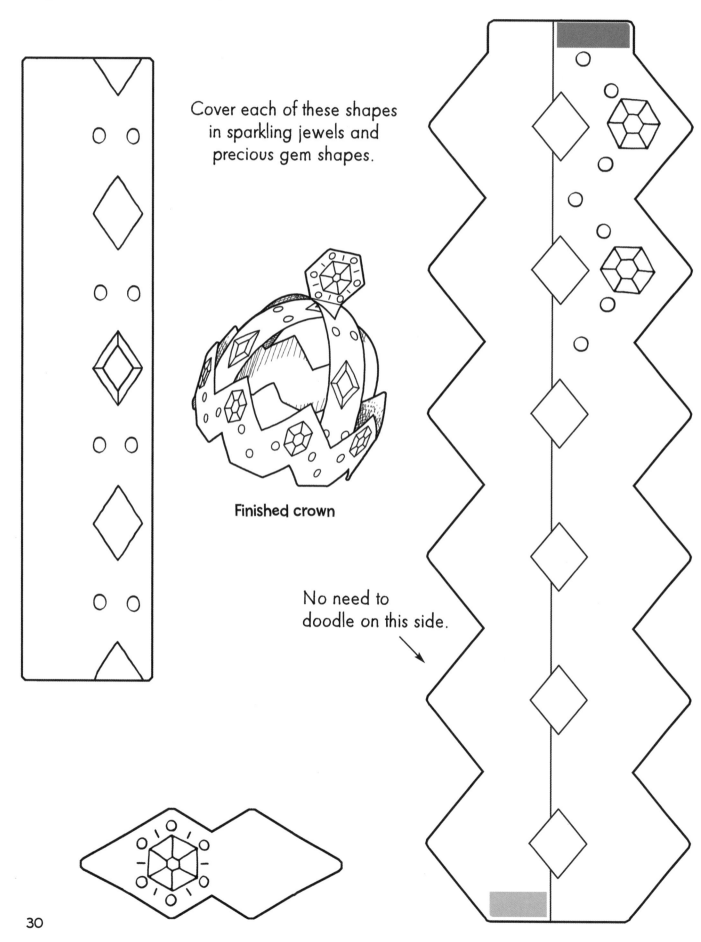

Finished crown

No need to doodle on this side.

Poodle Pooch

Add some curly, swirly, poodle hair to the shape on this page and the next, then cut out your poodle below.

1. Cut out the shape along the solid outside line, then score along each of the fold lines.

2. Fold all the dotted lines in the same direction, with the design on the outside, as shown.

Cover the areas pointed by arrows in pink or purple curly, swirly poodle hair.

3. Dab a spot of glue where indicated on the tab at the end of the poodle's tail.

4. Fix its tail to the glue positioning area on the back of the poodle's head.

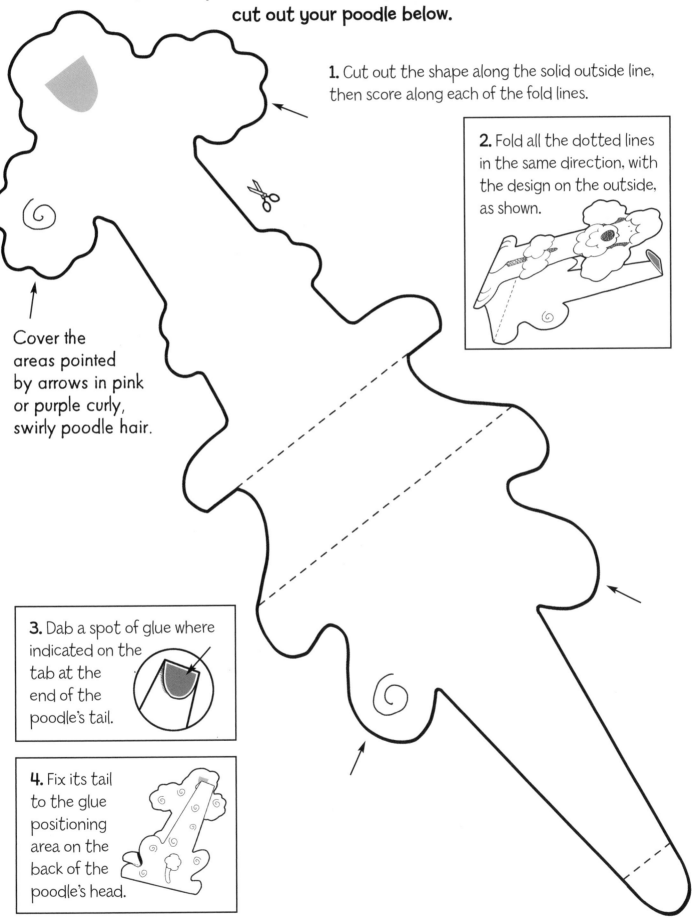

Poodle Pooch

Poodle owners often give their poodles a haircut to keep their coat short and neat. They sometimes even dye their dog's hair in crazy colors, such as purple or pink!

Cover this poodle in short, curly hair and color it in bright purple or pink.

Finished poodle

Dangling Tarantula

Give the tarantula shoes and furry legs on this page as well as the next, then cut it out below. You will also need a length of thread, measuring roughly 12 inches.

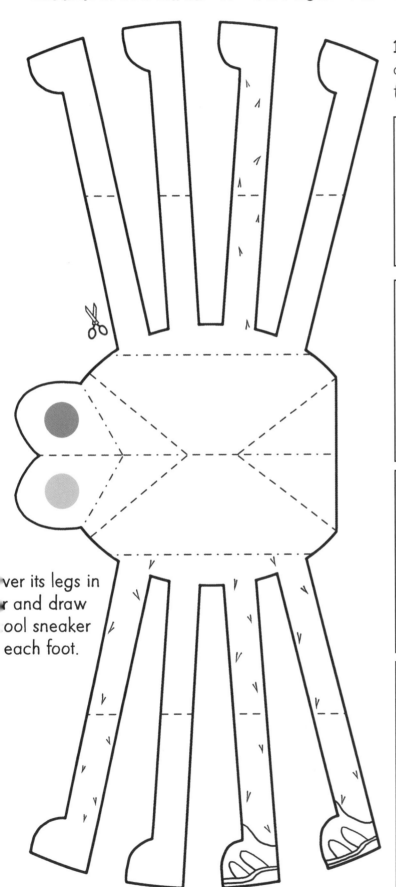

ver its legs in
r and draw
ool sneaker
each foot.

1. Cut out the shape along the solid outside line, then score along each of the fold lines.

2. Fold the shape in half along the central fold line, so that the design is on the outside.

3. Open out the shape as much as you need to (so that you can see the fold lines underneath), then pinch along the diagonal lines. Now push in the head and bottom ends, as shown.

4. Pinch the diagonal lines closest to the head and bend it up again, as shown. Add glue to the glue area, then squeeze both sides of the head together.

5. Bend the legs up toward the body, then bend them back at the knees.

6. Fix the thread to the middle of the back, then ask an adult to hang it from the ceiling of your bedroom.

Dangling Tarantula

Tarantulas are a species of spider with hair all over their bodies. They might look scary, but their bite is less harmful to a human than a honeybee's sting.

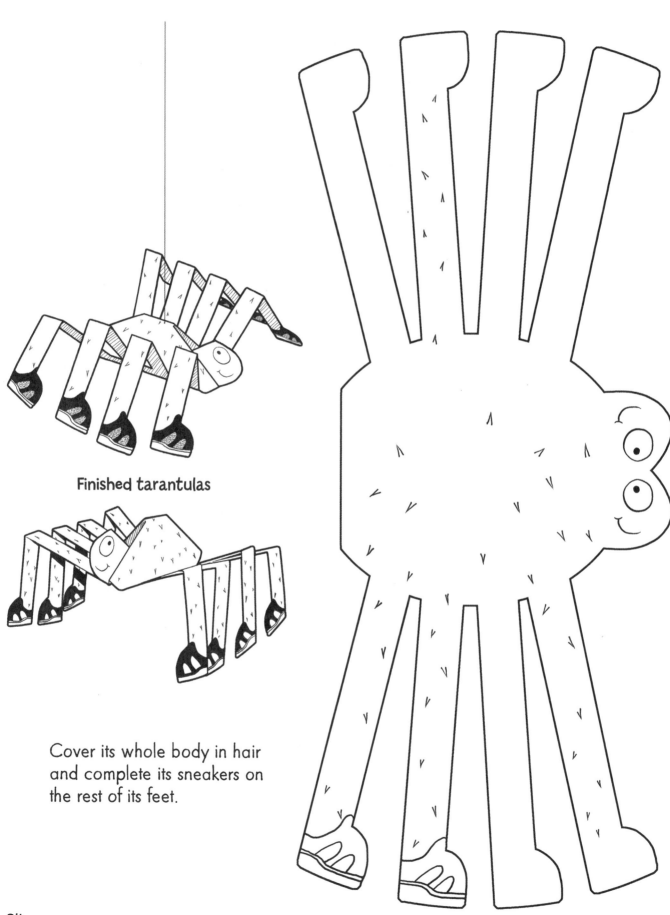

Finished tarantulas

Cover its whole body in hair and complete its sneakers on the rest of its feet.

Wrinkly Bulldog

Turn the page and doodle your design, then cut out your bulldog below.

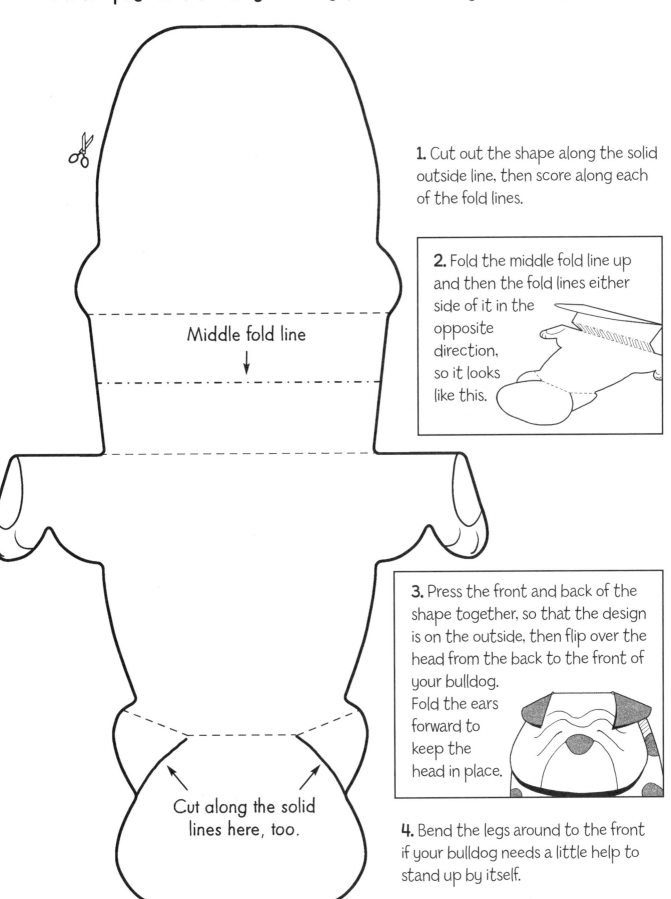

Middle fold line
↓

1. Cut out the shape along the solid outside line, then score along each of the fold lines.

2. Fold the middle fold line up and then the fold lines either side of it in the opposite direction, so it looks like this.

3. Press the front and back of the shape together, so that the design is on the outside, then flip over the head from the back to the front of your bulldog. Fold the ears forward to keep the head in place.

Cut along the solid lines here, too.

4. Bend the legs around to the front if your bulldog needs a little help to stand up by itself.

Wrinkly Bulldog

Bulldogs have big, wrinkly folds of skin covering their whole bodies. They also have funny, flat noses.

Cover the bulldog's body in wrinkly folds of skin and add patchy spots of brown hair, too.

Finished bulldog

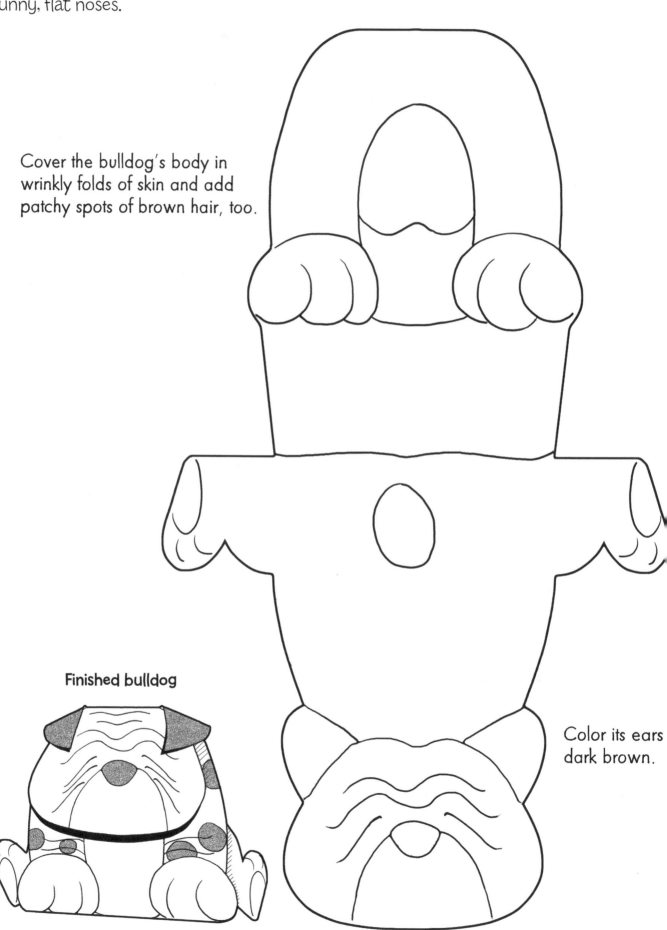

Color its ears dark brown.

Cock-a-Doodle-Doooo!

Complete the doodle design on this page and the next,
then cut out your cockerel below.

1. Cut out the shapes along the solid outside lines. Score along each fold line.

2. Make a small cut here along the solid line on shape A.

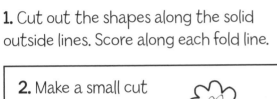

3. With the design on the outside, fold the shape along the central fold line, then fold the wings forward.

4. Line up shape B in the center behind shape A, then push the beak into the slit, as shown here.

5. Carefully open out the bird's body until it stands up by itself.

Give it a bright, red comb and a yellow beak.

Complete its pretty tail feathers and color them in green and blue.

Shape B

Color the wing feathers in shades of orange and red.

Shape A

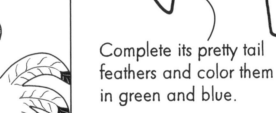
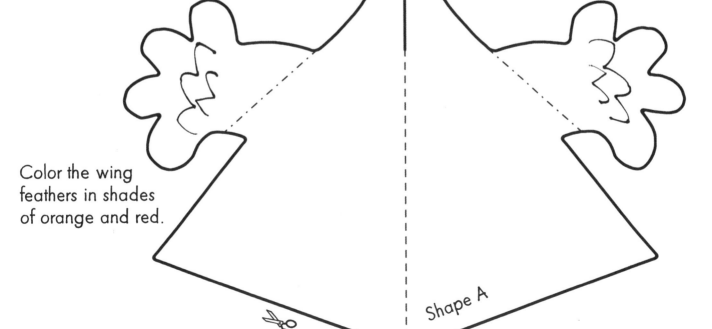
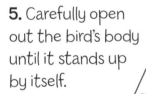

Cock-a-Doodle-Dooooo!

Cockerels are male chickens. They have a red, fleshy crest called a comb on the top of their heads and bright, beautiful tail feathers.

Give it a red, fleshy comb and a yellow beak.

Finish its long, beautiful tail feathers and color them in green and blue.

Finished cockerel

Color these wings in shades of orange and red.

Cover its body in short feathers.

Scaly Alligator

Finish the doodle design on this page and the next, then cut out the shapes below.

1. Cut out the shapes along the solid outside lines, then score along each of the fold lines.

Shape B

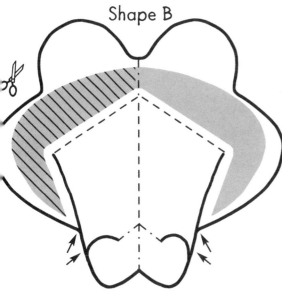

When you have cut out the head, cut along these heavy solid lines to make the snout and nostrils.

2. Fold shape A down the middle, with the tail side on the outside, then open the body out again like this, until it stands up by itself.

3. Pinch the diagonal lines on shape B (the head) and bend up the nose. Push back the tip.

4. Fold the head in half with the design on the inside. Put glue on the striped area on the body shape, and press the striped area of the head on to it. Hold it until it sticks.

5. Glue the other side of the head to the body, where marked.

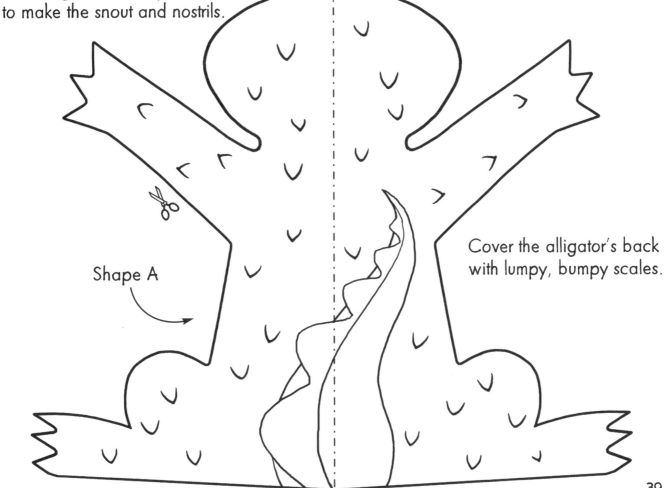

Shape A

Cover the alligator's back with lumpy, bumpy scales.

Scaly Alligator

Alligators' skins are covered in hard scales. They do not sweat through their skin. Instead they open their mouths to cool down, just like a dog does when it pants.

Finished alligator

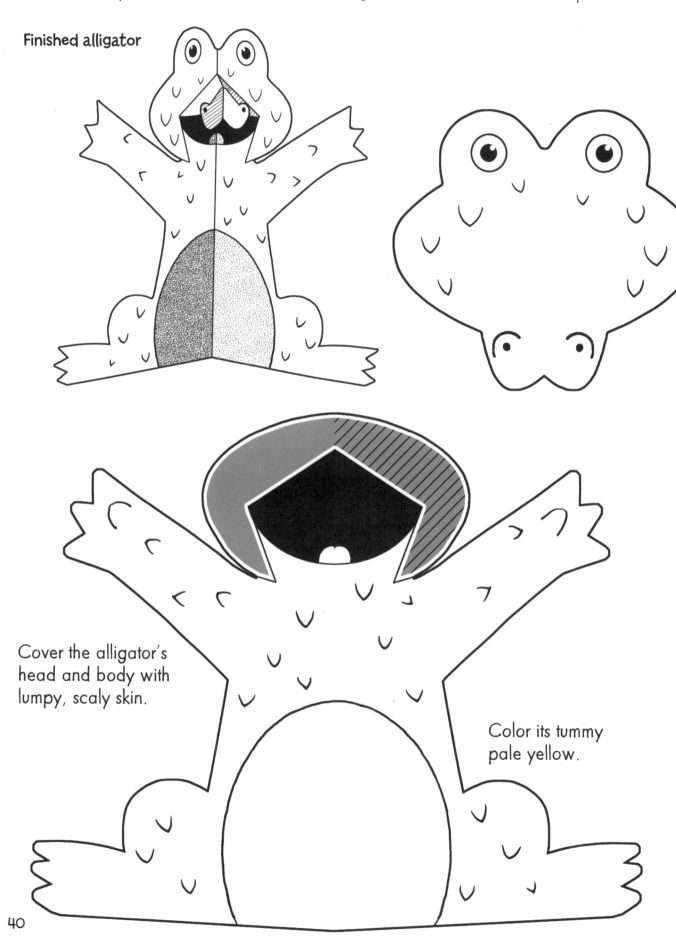

Cover the alligator's head and body with lumpy, scaly skin.

Color its tummy pale yellow.

Feathery Headdress

Turn the page and doodle your design, then cut out your headdress below.

1. Cut out these shapes along the solid outside lines.

2. Dab glue on to the dark gray areas on both strips, then glue the strips together to make one long strip. Now join the ends to make a circle, with your doodle design on the outside.

3. Glue one of the feather ends on the spot where two strips overlap, then glue on the other feather, so its end overlaps the first.

4. Glue the round shape on top of the ends of the feathers, making sure its design is on the outside, as shown above.

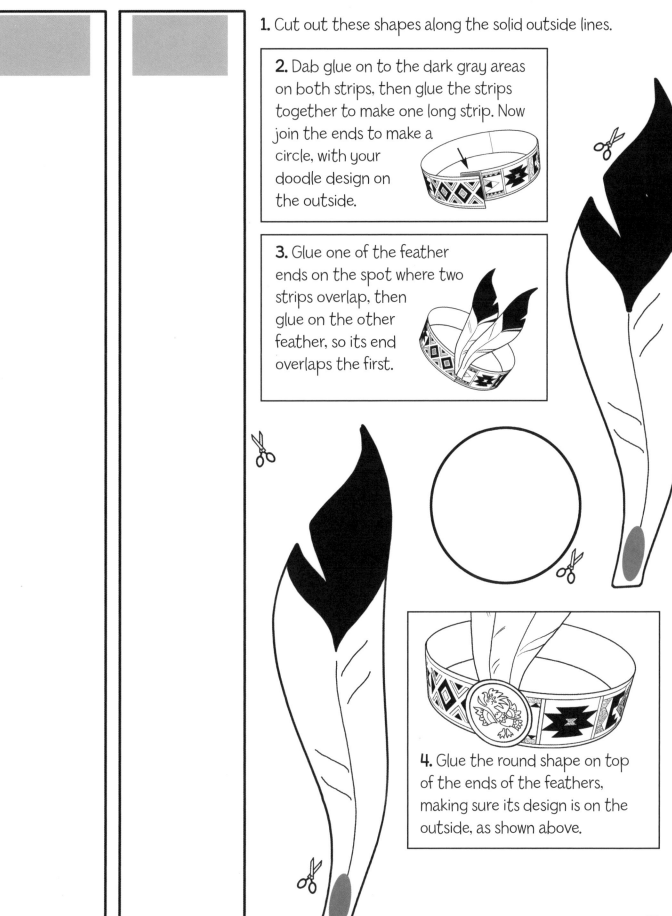

Feathery Headdress

Some Native American tribes wear beautiful headbands decorated with patterns made of shells, beads, and porcupine quills.

Finish the cool Native American pattern on these strips.

Add brightly colored feathers to the brilliant bird design inside the round shape below.

Finished headdress

Robots Rule!

Turn the page and doodle your design, then cut out your robot below.

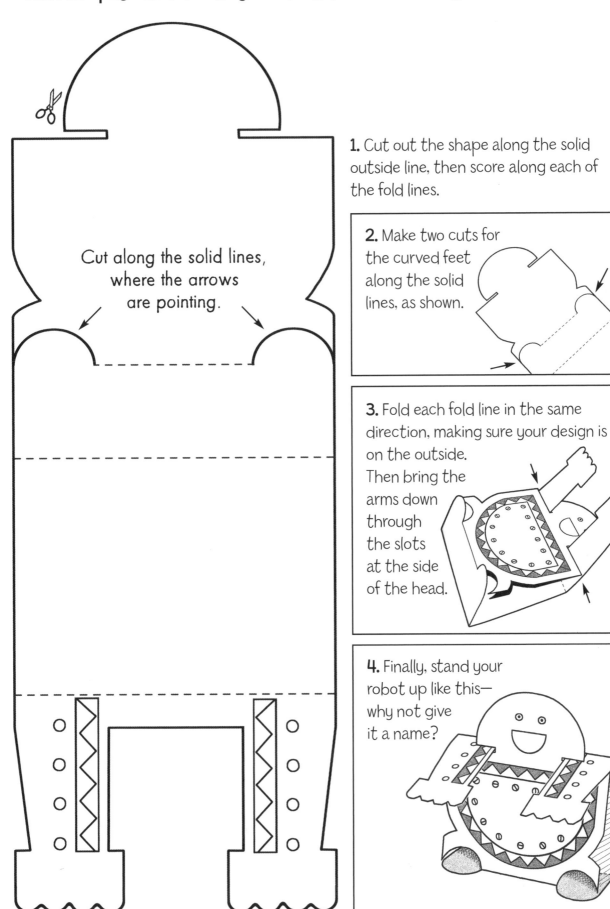

Cut along the solid lines, where the arrows are pointing.

1. Cut out the shape along the solid outside line, then score along each of the fold lines.

2. Make two cuts for the curved feet along the solid lines, as shown.

3. Fold each fold line in the same direction, making sure your design is on the outside. Then bring the arms down through the slots at the side of the head.

4. Finally, stand your robot up like this—why not give it a name?

Robots Rule!

Now's your chance to design your own robot. You can add as many control switches as you like, so that only you can command it.

Finish the nut-and-bolt design on the robot's bodywork.

Finished robot

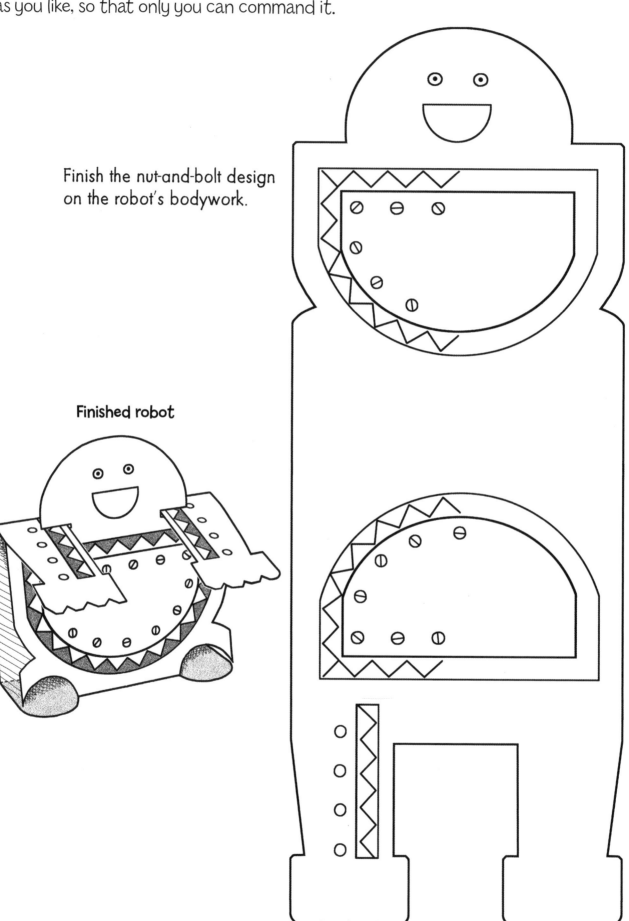

Kitty Photo Holder

Turn the page and doodle your design, then cut out your photo holder below.

1. Cut out the shape along the solid outside line, then score along each of the fold lines.

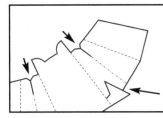

2. Make two short cuts at the top, as shown, and cut around the kitty's tail.

4. Cover the glue area in glue.

5. Fix the glued area to the glue positioning area on the other side of the cat's body, where marked.

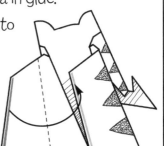

3. Fold all the fold lines in the same direction, except the folds in line with the short cuts. Fold these lines the other way.

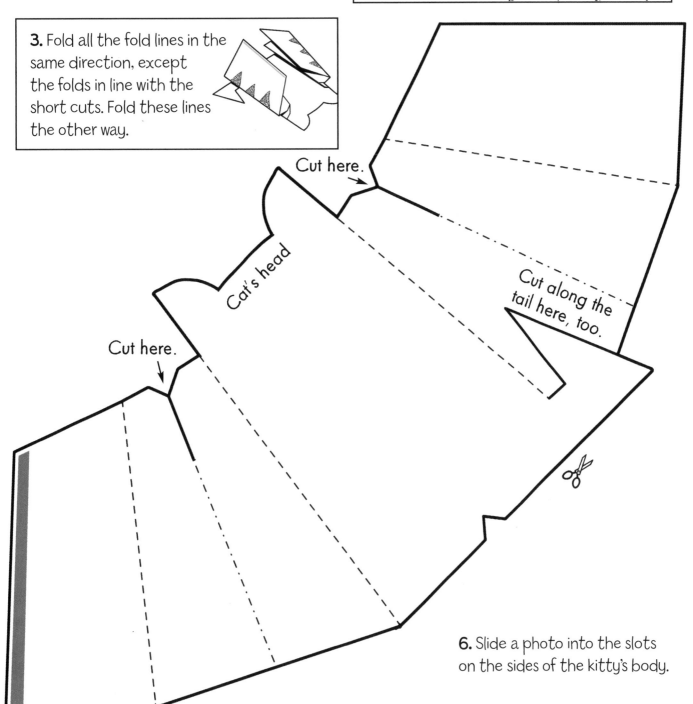

Cut here.

Cat's head

Cut here.

Cut along the tail here, too.

6. Slide a photo into the slots on the sides of the kitty's body.

Kitty Photo Holder

Why not make this cool, kitty photo holder for a member of your family? When you've finished making your photo holder, you could stick a photo of yourself inside the slots that you have made in the sides of its body and give it to someone special.

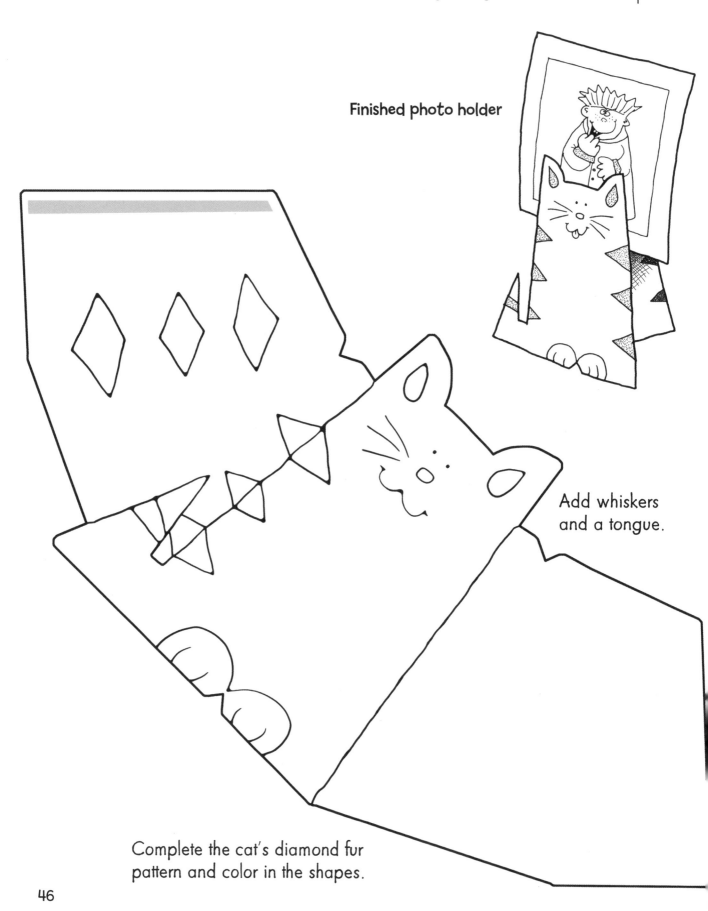

Finished photo holder

Add whiskers and a tongue.

Complete the cat's diamond fur pattern and color in the shapes.

Cool Kangaroo

**Complete the doodle design on this page and the next,
then cut out your kangaroo below.**

1. Cut out the shape along the solid outside line, then score along each of the fold lines.

2. Fold the shape in half along the central fold line, so that the design is on the outside.

3. Fold in the diagonal lines at the base of your kangaroo's tail and pinch along the reverse folds so that the tail comes up.

4. Crease along both sets of folds on the face.

5. Pinch the two sides of the face together and secure with a dab of glue to make a pointed nose.

Choose a favorite color and cover this side of the kangaroo with it.

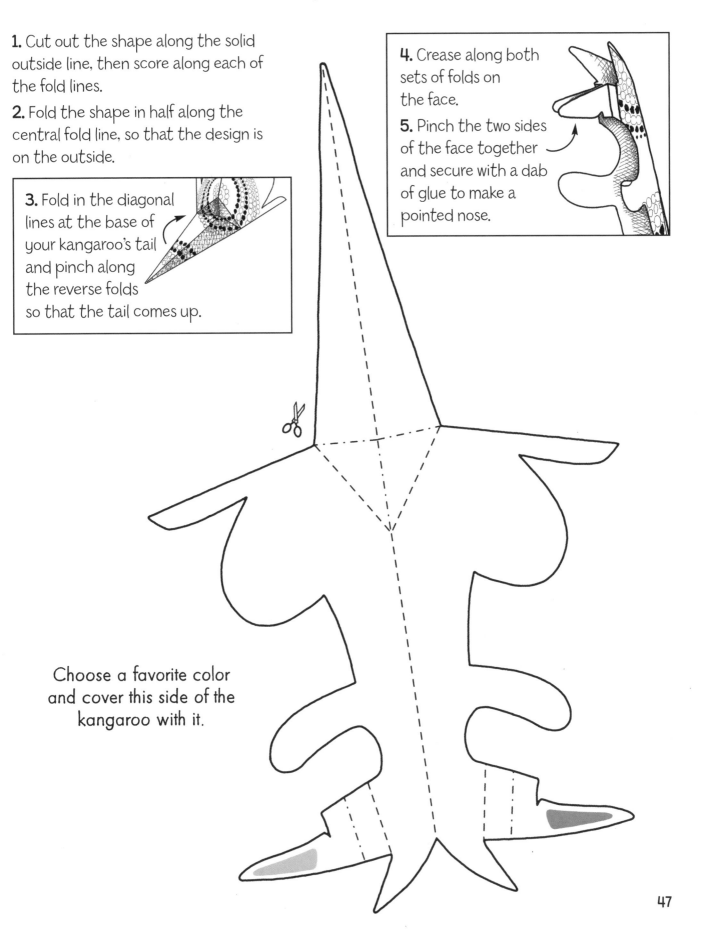

Cool Kangaroo

Kangaroos come from Australia. In Australia, Aboriginal people decorate their designs with lots of spots.

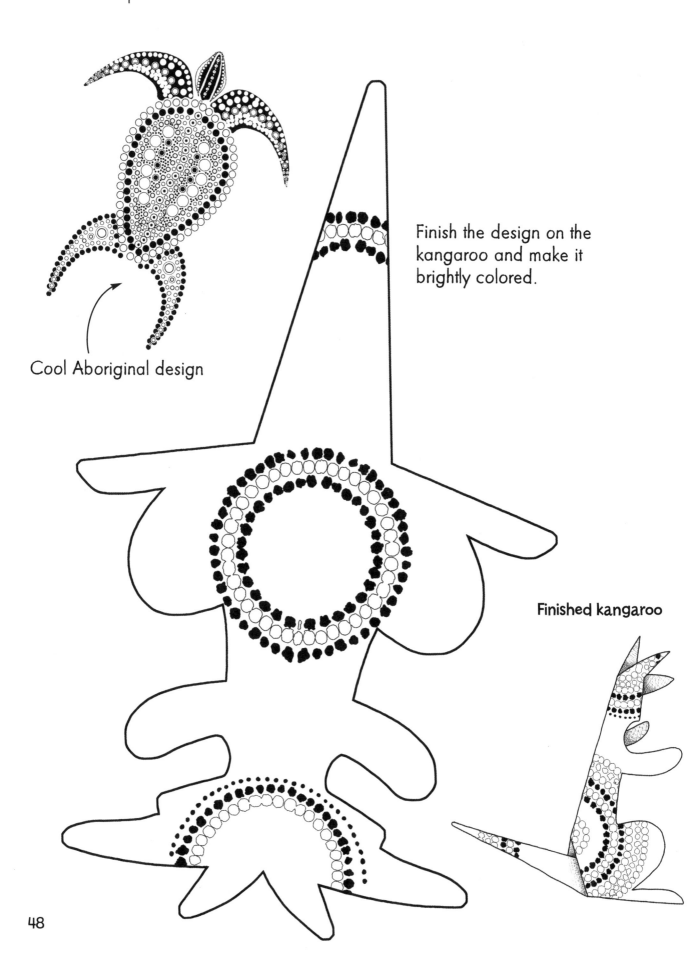

Cool Aboriginal design

Finish the design on the kangaroo and make it brightly colored.

Finished kangaroo

Perfect Penguin

Complete the doodle design on this page and the next, then cut out your penguin below.

1. Cut out the shape along the solid outside line, then score along each of the fold lines.

2. Fold the shape in half along the central fold line, so that the design is on the inside.

3. Cut along the solid line shown to form the beak.

4. Unfold the shape, then fold up the feet and make sharp creases.

5. Fold the penguin at the head so that the design is now on the outside.

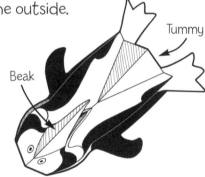

Tummy

Beak

6. Pinch along the diagonal lines closest to the body on the beak and tummy, then lift them both up so that they stick out from the body.

7. Fold the feet forward again, then fold the tail back until the penguin stands up by itself.

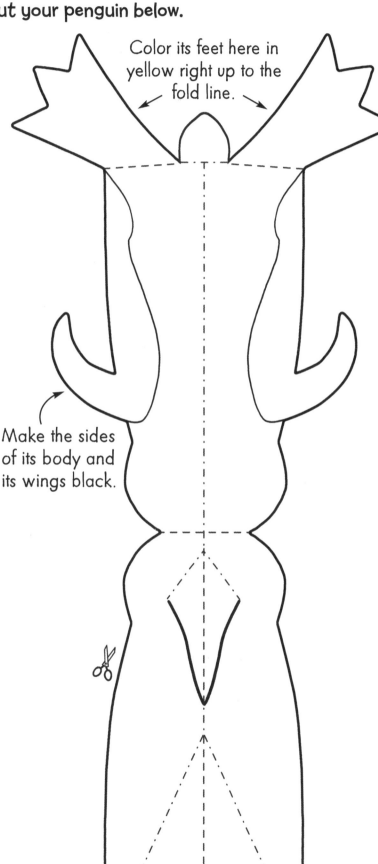

Color its feet here in yellow right up to the fold line.

Make the sides of its body and its wings black.

Perfect Penguin

Penguins are birds but they cannot fly. They use their wings like flippers to swim through the water to catch fish to eat.

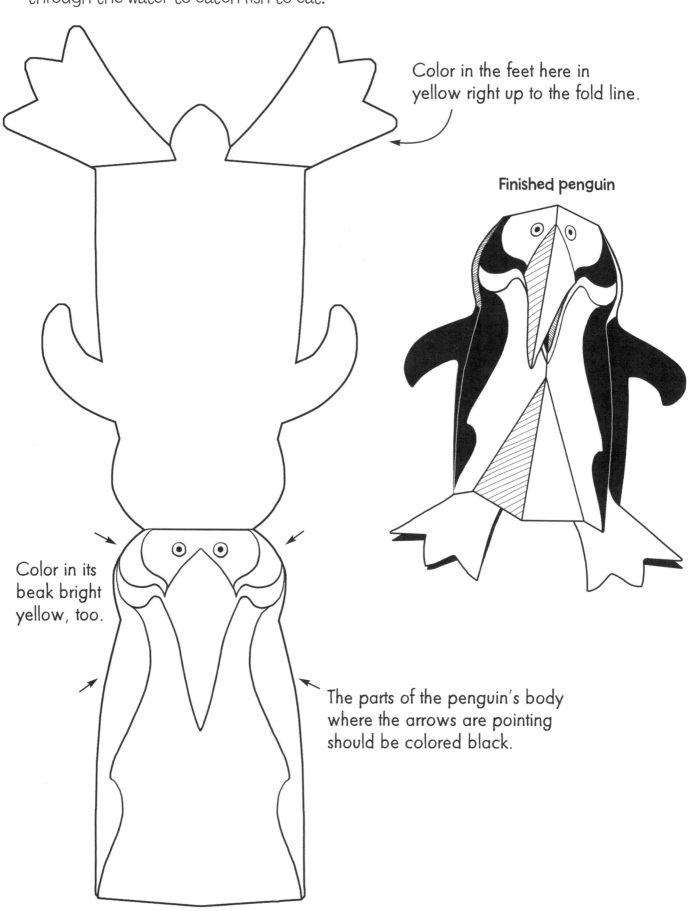

Color in the feet here in yellow right up to the fold line.

Finished penguin

Color in its beak bright yellow, too.

The parts of the penguin's body where the arrows are pointing should be colored black.

Cozy Cottage

Turn the page and doodle your design, then cut out your cottage below.

1. Cut out both shapes along the solid outside lines.

2. Bend each tab on shape B, toward the inside.

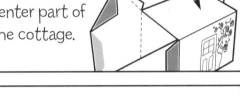

3. Cut along the solid lines of the door shape where shown.

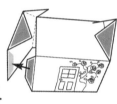

4. Fold over the center part of the cottage.

5. Cover each tab with glue, where marked. Fix tabs 1 and 2 to the inside of the cottage wall.

6. Fold shape A in half, so that the design is on the outside.

7. Stick tabs 3, 4, 5, and 6 to the inside of the roof.

8. Push the door open a little to make your cottage look welcoming.

Shape A

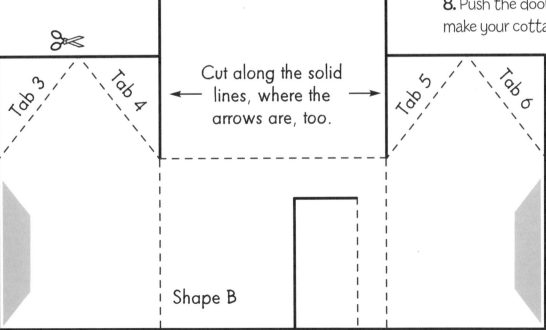

Tab 1

Tab 2

Tab 3

Tab 4

Cut along the solid lines, where the arrows are, too.

Tab 5

Tab 6

Shape B

Cozy Cottage

In the English countryside, cottages sometimes have a thatched roof. This is a roof that is made of bundles of straw or reeds instead of tiles.

Draw brown or yellow lines on the thatched roof to make thatch.

Finished cottage

Cover the cottage in vines and flowers and give the windows cute wooden shutters.

No need to doodle here or on the tabs.

Cool Motorcar

Turn the page and doodle your design, then cut out your motorcar below.

1. Cut out the shape along the solid outside line, then score along each of the fold lines.

2. Make small cuts, where shown.

3. Fold the shape in half along the central fold line at the top of the car, making sure the design is on the outside.

4. Fold along the fold lines, as shown. Put glue on the dark gray areas and stick the other sides down on top.

Cut along the solid lines, where the arrows are.

Cool Motorcar

Design a cool, old-fashioned motorcar complete with stylish spokes, huge hubcaps, and you in the driving seat!

Finished car

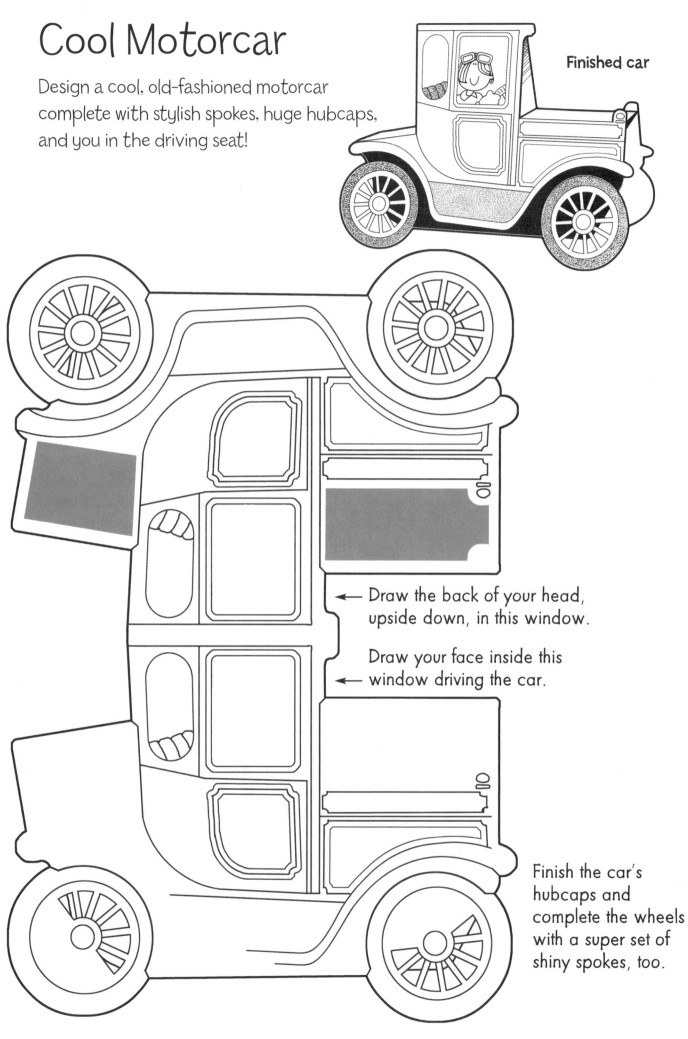

← Draw the back of your head, upside down, in this window.

Draw your face inside this
← window driving the car.

Finish the car's hubcaps and complete the wheels with a super set of shiny spokes, too.

Buzzing Beehive

Doodle stripes on the bees on this page and the next, then cut out each shape below. You will also need seven different lengths of thread and some sticky tape.

1. Cut out each shape along the solid outside lines. Cut slits along the solid lines inside the flaps, and on the bees' bodies and wings, too.

2. Dab some glue on to the tab, then line up the opposite edge with the tab and press together until it is stuck, forming a beehive shape.

3. Fold down the flaps and tape them flat on the inside and outside.

4. Tape a piece of thread to the center of the top of the beehive on the outside.

5. Slot a set of wings on to each bee's body.

6. Tape one end of a piece of thread to the top of each bee's body, and the other end to the inside of the beehive. Vary the lengths of thread, as shown opposite.

7. Ask an adult to hang your buzzing beehive mobile by the thread at the top of the hive, from the ceiling of your bedroom.

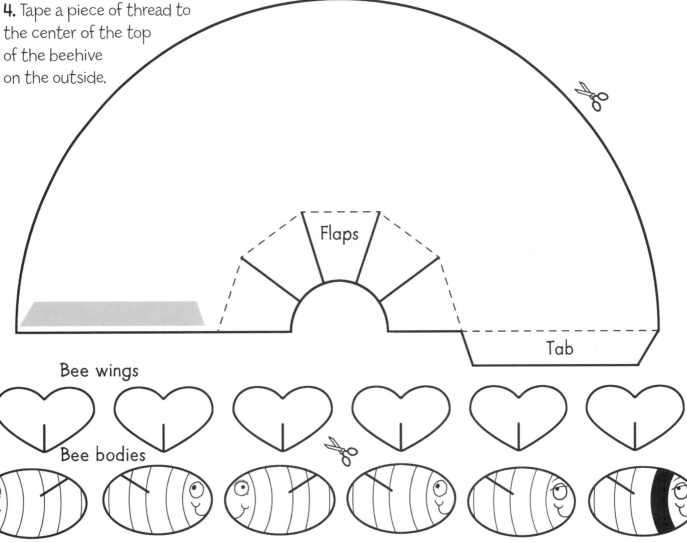

Flaps

Tab

Bee wings

Bee bodies

Buzzing Beehive

Honeybees collect nectar—a sweet, sugary liquid produced by flowers—and turn it into honey inside their hives. One hive can produce almost 60 pounds of honey in a season. . . . That's a lot of busy bees!

Finished beehive mobile

Complete the stripes on the bees' bodies below.

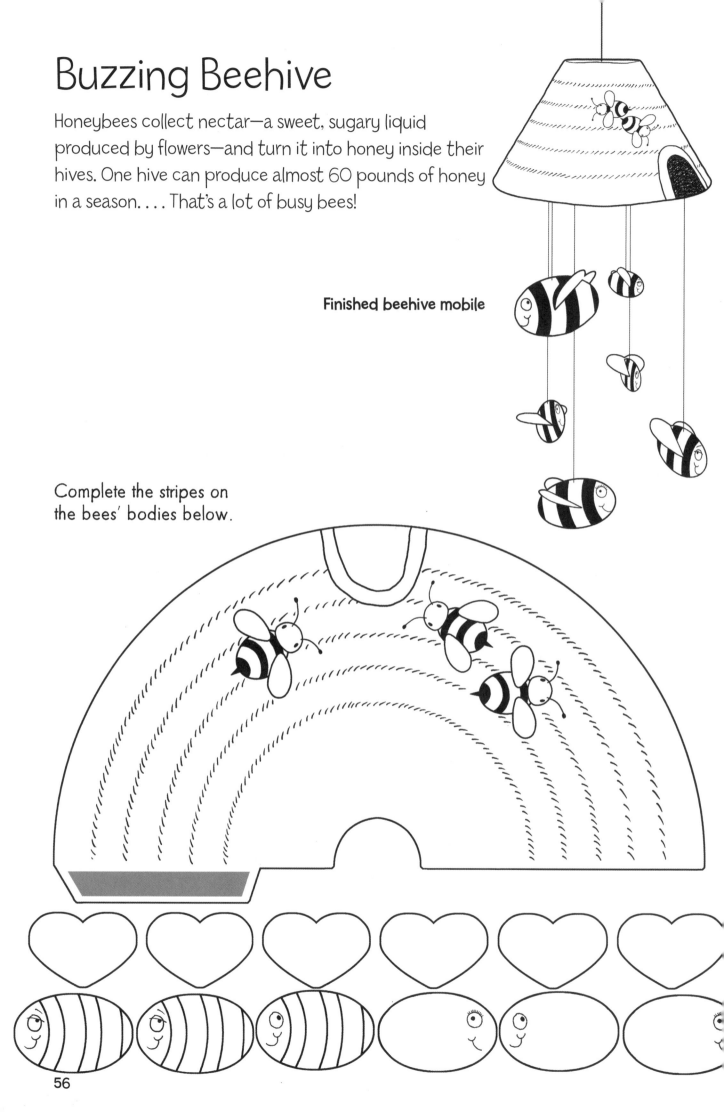

Lion Pop-Up Card

Turn the page and doodle your design, then cut out your card below.

1. Cut out both shapes along the solid outside line, then score along each of the fold lines.

2. Fold shape A in half along the central fold line, so that the design is on the inside, then make a small cut, where shown.

3. Cut out the shaded area and cut along the solid lines on either side of it.

4. Unfold the shape so the design is facing you. Fold up the top and bottom ends, pinching the folds to make them sharp.

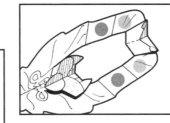

5. Bend forward the nose and bottom teeth, as shown here, pinching the folds again.

6. Add glue to the glue areas. Fold over these sections and stick them to the bottom of the lion's face, where marked.

7. Carefully fold the lion's head in half so that the design is on the inside and its mouth is open.

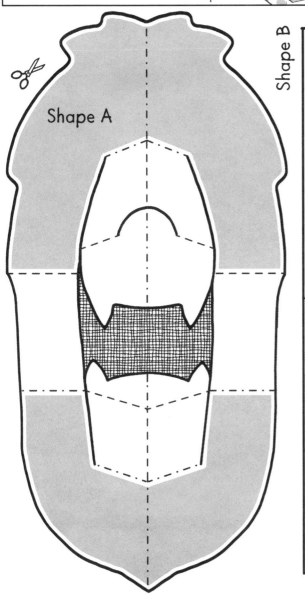

Shape A

Shape B

Lion Pop-Up Card

Give this cool card to a friend for his or her birthday. Write your birthday message on the outside of the card, then watch as the lion pops out when it is opened.

8. Add glue to the glue areas marked inside the card. Push the straight side of the lion's head firmly into the fold line of the card.

Carefully close the card and hold it closed until the glue has dried.

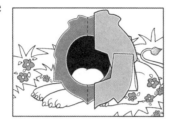

Finished card

Add more grass for the lion to hide behind in the scene below.

Cover its mane in curly hair.

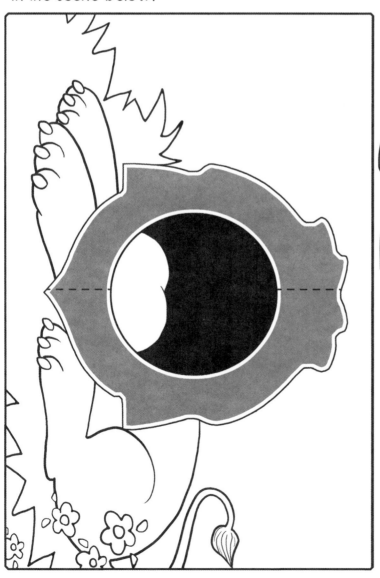

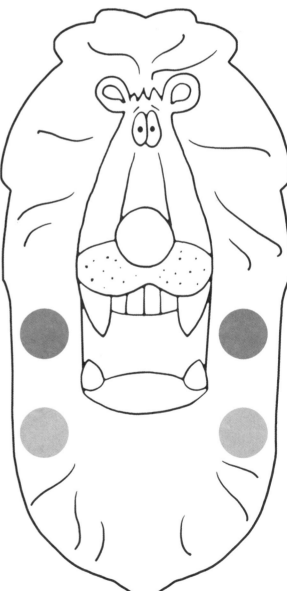

Fast Race Cars

Turn the page and doodle your designs, then cut out your race cars below.

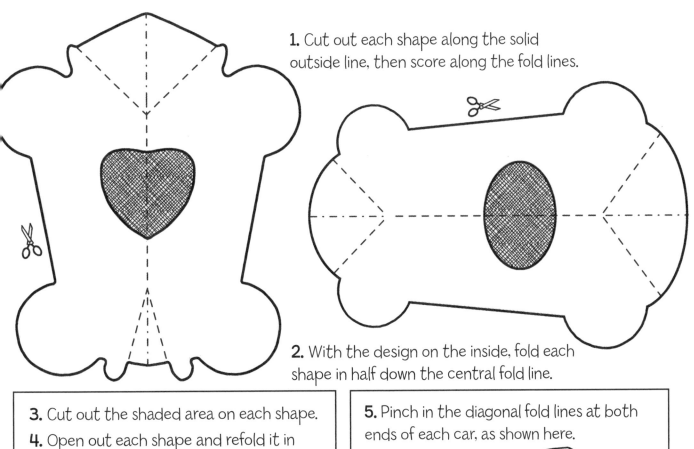

1. Cut out each shape along the solid outside line, then score along the fold lines.

2. With the design on the inside, fold each shape in half down the central fold line.

3. Cut out the shaded area on each shape.

4. Open out each shape and refold it in the opposite direction, so that the design is now on the outside.

5. Pinch in the diagonal fold lines at both ends of each car, as shown here.

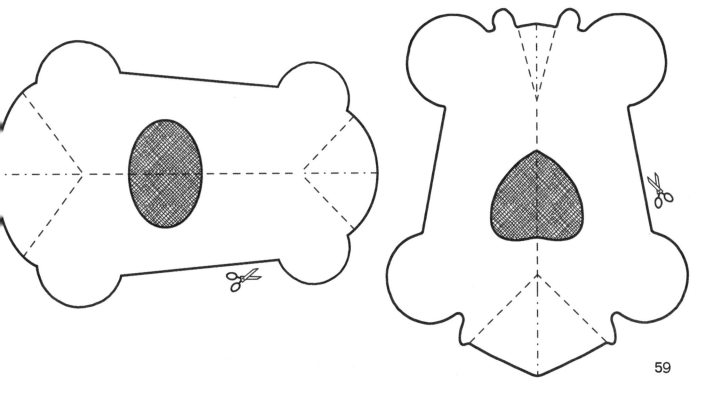

Fast Race Cars

On your mark ... get set ... go!

Turn these race cars into winners with a daring design.

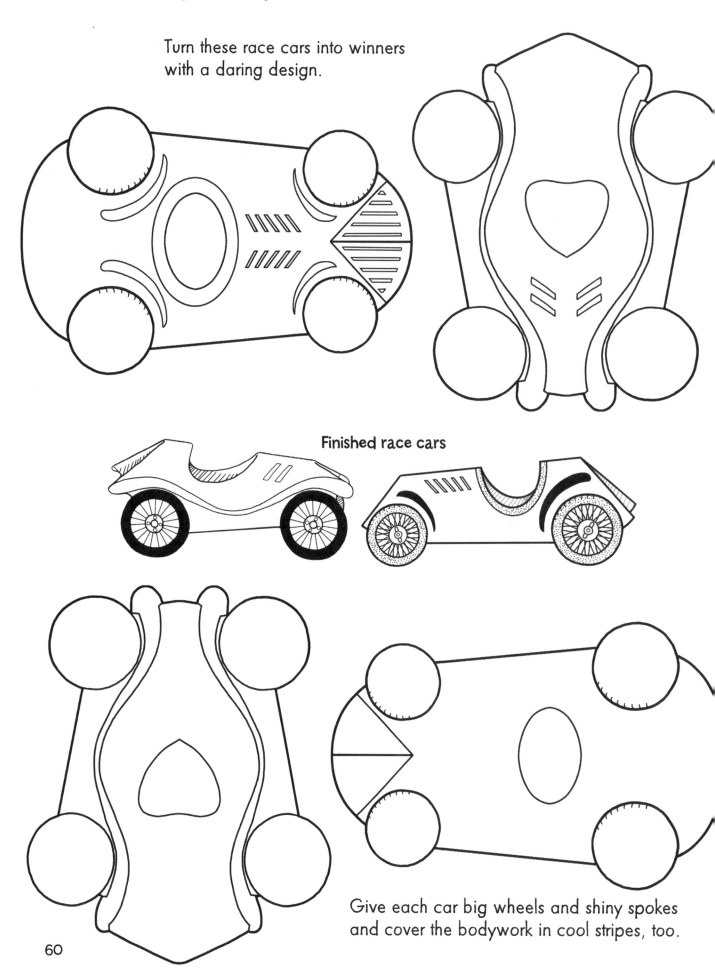

Finished race cars

Give each car big wheels and shiny spokes and cover the bodywork in cool stripes, too.

Magical Merry-Go-Round

Turn the page and doodle your design, then cut out your merry-go-round below. You will also need nine lengths of thread, measuring roughly 12 inches each.

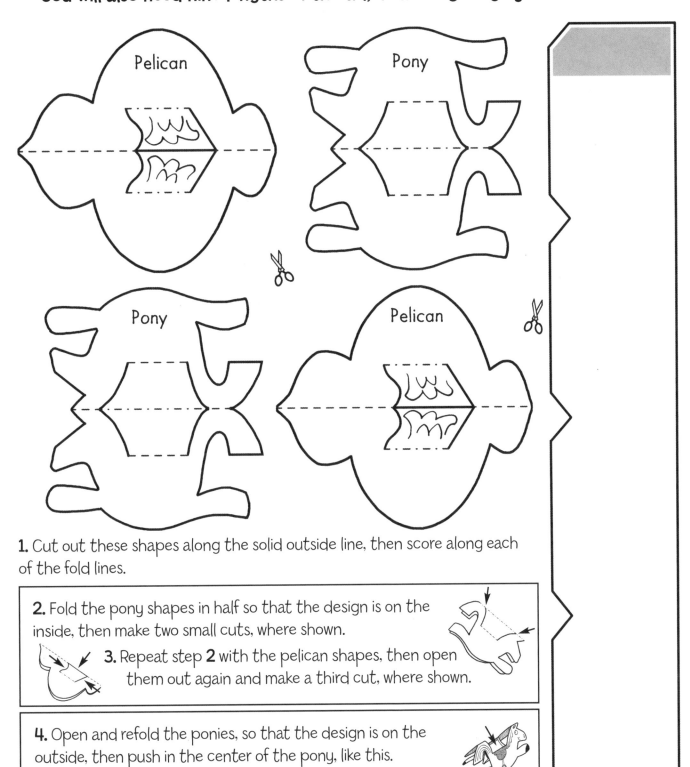

1. Cut out these shapes along the solid outside line, then score along each of the fold lines.

2. Fold the pony shapes in half so that the design is on the inside, then make two small cuts, where shown.

3. Repeat step 2 with the pelican shapes, then open them out again and make a third cut, where shown.

4. Open and refold the ponies, so that the design is on the outside, then push in the center of the pony, like this.

5. Fold the pelican back again so that the design is on the outside, then fold out the wings.

6. Add glue to the glue area on shape A, then join the ends together like this.

7. Tape thread to the top of both ends of each animal. Fix the other end of each thread to the inside edge of the circle shape.

Shape A

Magical Merry-Go-Round

These magical rides can be found in amusement parks. They are often covered in bright lights and play music as they turn around.

Doodle feathers and man on these animal shapes.

Create a colorful pattern on the blank spaces on this strip.

To hang your merry-go-round mobile, ask an adult to fix each end of the last piece of thread to the opposite sides of the circle and hang it up somewhere by a window, so you can watch it swing around in the breeze.

Finished merry-go-round